PONTIAC
MUSCLE CARS

Mike Mueller

MBI Publishing Company

First published in 1994 by MBI Publishing Company,
PO Box 1, 729 Prospect Avenue, Osceola,
WI 54020-0001 USA

MBI Publishing Company books are also available at
discounts in bulk quantity for industrial or sales-
promotional use. For details write to Special Sales
Manager at Motorbooks International Wholesalers &
Distributors, 729 Prospect Avenue, PO Box 1,
Osceola, WI 54020-0001 USA

Library of Congress Cataloging-in-Publication Data
Mueller, Mike.
    Pontiac muscle cars / Mike Mueller.
        p.   cm. — (Enthusiast color series)
    Includes index.
    ISBN 0-87938-863-3
    1. Pontiac automobile—History.   2. Muscle car—
United States—History.   I. Title. II. Series.
    TL215.P68M84   1994
    629.222—dc20   93-48648

On the front cover: According to *Motor Trend*, a 360
horsepower 1967 GTO was capable of a 14.09 second
quarter-mile at 101mph. This glorious example belongs
to Rob and Renee Lamarr of Cocoa Beach, Florida.

On the frontispiece: Optional Tri-Power feeds this 421
HO, helping boost horsepower to 376 at 5500rpm.

On the title page: A complete restyle in 1968 left little
of the previous generation GTO intact. The popular,
new look helped boost GTO production by nearly
6,000 units over 1967's total. Steve Maysonet of
Sunrise, Florida, owns this one.

On the back cover: Satellite Beach, Florida, resident
Morris Otto owns this very rare, first year Trans Am.
Fewer than 700 Trans Ams were built in 1969.

Printed in Hong Kong

Contents

Acknowledgments

I would like to extend my gratitude to Terry Spear of Terry's GTOs in Orlando, Florida, for his help and support in putting this project together. The efforts and enthusiasm of GTO fanatic Rob Lamarr of Cocoa Beach, Florida, were also appreciated. Appreciated as well were the cooperation and patience of the people who allowed their fine Pontiacs to be photographed for this book. In basic order of appearance, they are:

Bob and Mary McVeigh, Lake Park, Florida, 1959 Catalina convertible; Ronald Brauer, Crystal River, Florida, 1960 Ventura; Allan and Louise Gartzman, Skokie, Illinois, 1962 421 Super Duty Grand Prix; Henry Hart, Lakeland, Florida, 1962 421 Super Duty Catalina; Robert Gaito, Palm Harbor, Florida, 1963 Grand Prix; Allan Peranio, Coral Springs, Florida, 1965 2+2 convertible; Joe and Evelyn Alterizio, Brandon, Florida, 1967 Grand Prix convertible; Krieg Pruett, Altamonte Springs, Florida, 1964 GTO; Terry Spear, Orlando, Florida, 1966 GTO convertible; Rob and Renee Lamarr, Cocoa Beach, Florida, 1967 GTO; Linda Rutt, Palm Bay, Florida, 1967 GTO convertible; Steve Maysonet, Sunrise, Florida, 1968 GTO; Dan Andrews, Lakeland, Florida, 1971 GTO Judge; Don Maney, Orlando, Florida, 1972 GTO; Mike Webb, 1967 Firebird 400, Longwood, Florida; Jerry Ellis, Longwood, Florida, 1968 Firebird 400 convertible; Morris Otto, Satellite Beach, Florida, 1969 Trans Am; Dick Goodell, Lake Worth, Florida, 1969 Firebird 400 convertible; Terry Spear, Orlando, Florida, 1970 Firebird Formula 400; Jeff Jolley, Champaign, Illinois, 1970 Trans Am; Ed and Cindy Verner, Plant City, Florida, 1972 Trans Am.

Chapter 1

Power and Pizzazz
Pontiac's Performance Legacy

For more than thirty years, General Motors' Pontiac Motor Division truly has been the home of excitement. Once the builder of mundane cars grandpa was proud to drive, Pontiac pulled an about-face in the late 1950s, thanks mostly to the arrival of General Manager Semon E. "Bunkie" Knudsen in 1956.

General Motors had launched the Pontiac division in January 1926. The division's purpose was to fill the price gap between affordable Chevrolet and middle-class Oldsmobile. Named after the revered Ottawa Indian chief who had once ruled over all of the Midwest tribes of the Great Lakes region, Pontiac automobiles displayed their Native American imagery with pride. They ably filled the Chevy/Olds gap, using durability and dependability as main selling points.

By the mid-1950s, however, winning over car buyers was no longer the same game it had been in the 1930s and 1940s—suddenly power and pizzazz became major attractions.

In 1955, Chevrolet proved that putting affordable performance into the hands of young, excitable buyers could boost sales, both today's and tomorrow's. Somewhat ironically, the ball-stud rocker arm arrangement, which had helped make Chevy's first overhead-valve V-8 so hot, had been borrowed from Pontiac's design for its first OHV V-8, a modern power-

When Roger Huntington took his seat next to Jim Wangers behind the wheel of a 1962 Super Duty in January 1962, he didn't know quite what to expect. As he told it in *Motor Trend*, "Boom . . . Wangers got into that big Poncho, and we *went*. Low gear was a rubber-burning fishtail. A snap shift to second at 5000rpm, and 60mph came up in a bit over five seconds. The bellowing open exhausts rattled the whole countryside. Second and third gears almost tore my head off. Then across the finish line in high at 5300—stopping the watch at 13.9 [seconds] and 107mph!" In conclusion, Huntington called the Super Duty "a terrific piece of automobile. I'm still shaking."

Like the surgeon general's warning on a pack of Marlboro's, this badge foretold bad things for unwary stoplight challengers in the early 1960s. Powering Pontiac's full-sized boulevard bruisers, the 421 big-block first appeared in awesome Super Duty form in late 1961.

plant that also debuted in 1955. Pontiac would not lose the jump on the young crowd again. In 1956, Knudsen was promoted to Pontiac General Manager and stated his guiding philosophy: "You can sell a young man's car to an old man, but you'll never sell an old man's car to a young man."

With that precept, Knudsen began to build a young man's car company by surrounding himself with young car guys. In September 1956, just two months after he took Pontiac's general manager position, Knudsen hired Oldsmobile's Elliot "Pete" Estes as his chief engineer and Packard's John DeLorean as director of advanced engineering. At the same time, Knudsen opened PMD's "backdoor" to legendary Daytona Beach speed merchant

Smokey Yunick, whose race-proven practices greatly benefited Knudsen both at Pontiac and later at Chevrolet.

One of Knudsen's first moves towards changing PMD's image was to delete the traditional Silver Streaks from 1957 Pontiac hoods. Knudsen also eliminated much of the Native American imagery that had been a Pontiac trademark for three decades. The new general manager succeeded in cutting most of the ties with the division's stoic past; 1959's debut of the Wide Track Pontiacs severed any remaining ties. These models not only helped establish all-new industry trends, but also kicked off a fresh, exciting image that carried Pontiac to prominence in the 1960s.

While the somewhat sexy, certainly sleek Wide Tracks were basking in the glory of *Motor Trend's* Car of the Year honors, Pontiac's hot-blooded engineers were hard at work developing their Super Duty performance parts program. Initially, the Super Duty project was an underground, covert operation thanks to 1957's infamous Automobile Manufacturers Association ban on factory racing activities. Pontiac's project quickly escalated into a full-fledged competition program with intimidating results, including total domination of NASCAR's Grand National stock car circuit in 1961 and 1962.

Poised to rise head and shoulders above the other manufacturers in Detroit's performance arena, Pontiac's power brokers suddenly found themselves chopped off at the knees. In January 1963, GM chiefs sent down an edict from corporate headquarter's fourteenth floor ordering all factory-supported racing efforts to cease immediately. Perhaps that edict was a blessing in disguise, however, for it helped redirect Pontiac's focus from the racetrack to the street.

Despite heavy disapproval from the fourteenth floor, Pontiac rolled out its iconoclastic GTO in 1964. The GTO was a groundbreaking performance machine that set the tempo for what would become Detroit's muscle car era. Far from being high-tech, PMD's "GeeTO Tiger" was simply a big engine in a light car. It was also readily available, relatively affordable, and really fast.

As *Car and Driver*'s David E. Davis wrote in

Following in the fabled footsteps of Pontiac's 389 and 421 big-blocks, 1967's 428 V-8 emerged at a time when full-sized performance was on the wane across Detroit. Best suited for running power steering pumps and air conditioners under Grand Prix hoods, the torquey 428 was still a force to be reckoned with in 376 horsepower HO form.

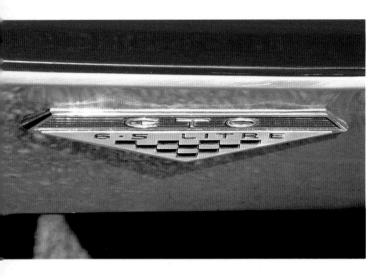

Although early 1960s street racers undoubtedly couldn't have cared less about the metric system, gearheads who couldn't translate this badge to Yankee terms ended up eating dust in a hurry. From 1964 through 1967, Pontiac's front-running GTO relied on PMD's 6.5 liter, 389 cubic inch big-block V-8 to do all the talking

a January 1975 testimonial to the Goat's honored contribution to American performance history:

> The real difference between the GTO and everything else of its type at the time was muscle. Back in 1964, Ford was pumping millions of dollars into a vast promotion called "Total Performance," and all the racing entrepreneurs in the country were benefiting hugely from massive transfusions of Ford money. But Ford couldn't make it happen on the street. Not so, GTO. The basic GTO with the basic hot set-up just let you climb inside and then asked you, "How far, how soon,

daddy?" [NASCAR driver] Fred Lorenzen might run like hell in his Holman-Moody Ford, but somehow the [Fords] you could buy never made your eyes bug out. Pontiac, on the other hand, put it right out there on the street; and the seekers of truth along Woodward Avenue and Ventura Boulevard understood.

Of course, performance phenomena like the GTO would have never made the scene had PMD not been led by a succession of gearheads in the 1960s. As engineers first and corporate executives second, Estes and DeLorean followed in Knudsen's footsteps as PMD's general managers. Estes became general manager in November 1961 once Knudsen moved over to Chevrolet; DeLorean in July 1965 after Estes also joined Chevrolet. If Estes had not stuck his neck out over an unproven concept, corporate killjoys would have never allowed the GTO to upset their entrenched apple cart. DeLorean's insistence that Pontiac build a true sports car would prove just as important to the later Fire-

Right
Pontiac chief John DeLorean always wanted a true PMD sports car—what he got in 1967 was the sporty Firebird, a Pontiac pony car that did its Camaro cousin one better in both looks and handling. Fitted with the optional 400 cubic inch big-block, the Firebird was a cinch to put Ford's Mustang out to pasture. In 1968, the 400 also replaced the veteran 389 as the GTO's heart and soul.

bird's existence and help differentiate that car from the rest of Detroit's pony car herd.

Although Estes and DeLorean's supporting cast was full of great names, two stand out: Jim Wangers and Ace Wilson. Full-time ad exec, part-time hell-bent-for-leather drag racer, Wangers joined McManus, John and Adams (Pontiac's advertising agency) in June 1958 after having helped promote Chevy's "Hot One" image as a Campbell-Ewald adman in 1955. A firm believer in the powers of performance in selling cars, Wangers' work on the marketing end may have meant as much to Pontiac's muscle car legacy as the actual design and production of the cars themselves.

One of the first feathers in Wangers' cap came in 1959 when he hooked up with Ace Wilson's Royal Pontiac dealership in Royal Oak, Michigan; that relationship served as a research and development avenue of sorts for Pontiac's performance projects. Chevrolet had

Don Yenko, Ford had Carroll Shelby, and PMD had Ace Wilson and his Royal Bobcat Pontiacs, winners on both road and track. The Royal Bobcat label first appeared in 1961 on a hot Catalina super stocker and later graced a host of equally hot GTOs.

As for the Firebird, its 1967 debut kicked off an exciting performance bloodline that remains pumping strong today. Whether in Euro-style six-cylinder Sprint, muscular Formula 400, or legendary Trans Am forms, Pontiac's pony car has always ranked among Detroit's greatest movers and shakers. The famed Trans Am is the only model from any auto maker to have run nonstop from its beginnings in the classic muscle car era up to the present, retaining its high-profile performance image all the way.

Led by an all-new Trans Am in 1994, Pontiac clearly hasn't lost a step when it comes to building excitement.

Pontiac's 455 cubic inch HO big-block was indicative of just how wild Detroit's horsepower race got before the axe fell in 1971. The evaporation of GM's 400 cubic inch displacement limit for its 1970 intermediates meant that the 455 could be ordered as a GTO option. Pontiac's torque monster also became the sole powerplant for the Trans Am in both 1971 and 1972.

Chapter 2

Warriors
Wide Track Style, Super Duty Might, and Grand Prix Class

Pontiac Motor Division had already been making moves, though slowly, towards a modern image before Bunkie Knudsen—GM's youngest-ever divisional general manager—came on board on July 1, 1956. Like Chevrolet, Pontiac had introduced its first overhead-valve V-8 in 1955, a powerplant nearly ten years in the making. Although Pontiacs in 1955 and 1956 suddenly had modern power, they still lacked pizzazz; much of PMD's image still relied on old-fashioned practices. While Knudsen couldn't transform that image overnight, he could update it a piece at a time.

His first targets were the twin chrome trim strips applied to Pontiac hoods. Knudsen's father, William Knudsen, had first applied the strips in 1935 when *he* was Pontiac's general manager. The elder Knudsen's goal had been merely to turn a few customers' heads, but the "Silver Streaks" soon became a Pontiac trademark, along with its Native American imagery. By 1956, however, father no longer knew best

and son was convinced he had to cut ties to the past.

"We had to get rid of that 'Indian concept,' " claimed Knudsen in an interview some years later. "No reflection on the American Indian, but old chief Pontiac had been associated in the public mind with a prosaic, family-toting sedan from the time Pontiacs were first built." Even as the new 1957 models were nearing production, Bunkie Knudsen made the decision to do away with the Silver Streaks.

He also decided to offer an alarming new Pontiac for 1957, a car young Bunkie hoped would turn a head or two. Introduced in Febru-

The eye-catching 1963 Grand Prix featured clean sheet metal stripped of the long trim common to the base Catalina and longer Bonneville models; "Completely naked of chrome," in the words of *Motor Trend*'s Bob McVay. Pontiac's second-edition Grand Prix found 72,959 buyers, more than twice as many as the previous year.

Coined by Milt Colson, of McManus, John and Adams, Pontiac's advertising agency, the Wide Track label was a natural for the all-new 1959 Pontiacs. At 64in, the Wide Track cars were 5in wider at the wheels compared to their 1958 predecessors. The modern, skinny-whitewall tires are incorrect owner-installed equipment.

ary, the exclusive 1957 Bonneville convertible was a high-profile, high-priced performance showboat powered by a 310 horsepower 347 cubic inch V-8 fed by a Rochester fuel-injection system. The fully loaded Bonneville kicked off a new PMD tradition of conjuring up established, race-bred imagery when naming new models. The Bonneville also established Ponti-ac as a force to be reckoned with in Detroit's horsepower race. Few customers, however, got the chance to launch one out of the blocks, as only 630 were built.

Window dressing or not, Knudsen's fuel-injected Bonneville was just one step in a rapidly escalating progression of power. Pontiac's first true performance engine, a NASCAR-

Introduced in 287 cubic inch form in 1955, Pontiac's versatile OHV V-8 offered ample room for future growth. Enlarged to 317 cubic inches in 1956, 347 cubic inches in 1957, and 370 cubic inches in 1958, PMD's V-8 was enlarged again to 389 cubic inches for Wide Track duty in 1959. Pictured is the Bonneville 389, which, when backed by the optional Hydra-Matic automatic transmission, used 10:1 pistons and a Carter four-barrel carburetor to pump out 300 horsepower. When mated to the standard three-speed manual trans, the Bonneville 389's compression dropped to 8.6:1, with a corresponding output decrease to 260 horsepower.

inspired 285 horsepower 317 cubic inch V-8 with dual four-barrel carburetors, had appeared in January 1956 as a limited-edition option.

When Knudsen brought former Olds engineer Pete Estes aboard in September, he also received Estes' knowledge of Oldsmobile's soon-to-arrive J2 triple-carb setup. In 1957, Pontiac debuted its optional Tri-Power atop an enlarged 347 cubic inch V-8. Top output for the Tri-Power 347 was 317 horsepower. In 1958, both displacement and maximum output increased to 370 cubic inches and 330 horsepower, respectively.

With the engineering groundwork laid, it was left to the design crew to hold up their end, which they did in award-winning fashion. As the first totally new Pontiac to follow hot on the heels of another totally new Pontiac, the 1959 Wide Tracks were longer, lower, and, naturally, wider than their predecessors. They established a trend all GM divisions would adopt. Underpinning Joe Schemansky's Strato-Star styling were a reported forty-seven new mechanical features. That was enough to convince *Motor*

Right
Offered as a trim package on the Catalina four-door Vista sedan and two-door hardtop, the Ventura option was introduced in 1960, further endearing buyers who preferred a little pizzazz in their daily transportation. Included in the deal was exterior identification, deluxe wheel covers, a sport steering wheel, and distinctive tri-tone seats done in Morrokide (Pontiac's imitation leather). In this case, the wheel covers were superseded by Pontiac's attractive eight-lug aluminum wheels. Pontiac built 27,577 Ventura hardtops in 1960.

Beneath that large, black air cleaner are three Rochester two-barrel carburetors, the mixers that made up Pontiac's famed Tri-Power option, first offered in 1957. This 1960 Tri-Power 389 V-8 was rated at 333 horsepower.

Trend to honor Pontiac with its coveted "Car of the Year" award. When introducing his Wide Tracks, Knudsen bragged that "Pontiac had broken all bonds of traditional styling and engineering with the most progressive changes in our division's history." Those changes resulted in an amazing 77 percent sales increase over 1958's recession-racked results.

According to some Pontiac performance experts, 1959 was also the year the fabled Super Duty legacy was born. No one is sure who first used the Super Duty moniker or exactly when it was first used. Most PMD followers point to the December 1959 release of numerous high-performance parts, which were intended for 1960 NASCAR competition, as the Super Duty debut. Fireball Roberts' 1960 Pontiac—armed with a 348 horsepower 389 Super Duty V-8 (a 363 horsepower Tri-Power variety was also built)—announced that debut in February with a then-incredible 155mph lap around Daytona's   h banks. Pontiac's racing dominance co   ed into the fall as Jim Wangers pil   a Super Duty "Poncho" to

Super Stock and Top Stock Eliminator victories at drag racing's Labor Day weekend NHRA Nationals in Detroit.

Maximum Super Duty 389 output jumped to 368 horsepower early in 1961, a year when Pontiacs would win thirty of fifty-two NASCAR races. Then, just before the NHRA Nationals in Indianapolis, PMD engineers introduced a grossly underrated 373 horsepower 421 cubic inch Super Duty V-8. Only about a dozen were delivered to professional drag racers, inspiring NHRA rule-makers to step in. In the interest of fairness, NHRA officials specified that a performance package had to be offered to the public as a regular production option to remain legal for stock-class competition on the drag strip.

Pontiac's answer in 1962 was a special run of even more powerful 421 SD V-8s offered as factory options for Catalina sedans and hardtops, as well as Grand Prix sport coupes. A certified super stock screamer, the 1962 421 Super Duty was based on a beefy four-bolt block stuffed full of 11.1:1 Mickey Thompson forged aluminum pistons, a forged steel crank and a radical "#10 McKellar" solid-lifter cam, the latter feature named for its designer, engineer Malcolm McKellar.

Also included were twin Carter four-barrels, an eight-quart oil pan, and a pair of free-flowing cast-iron headers incorporating convenient cutouts for wide-open running. Output was quoted as 405 horsepower, although veteran road tester Roger Huntington claimed in his famous May 1962 *Motor Trend* review that actual power production was closer to 465 horsepower.

To top off the Super Duty package, Pontiac also offered various lightweight parts, including a hood, front bumper, fenders, inner fenders, and radiator brackets, all stamped out of alu-

If it wasn't clear Pontiac was aiming its products at the youth market, the 1960 Ventura trim package's tri-tone interior was quick evidence. The steering wheel and an electric clock were also included with the Ventura option.

23

Like the GTO to follow, Pontiac's first Grand Prix was set apart from the standard 1962 Catalina model it was based on by the addition of an exclusive blacked-out grille. Five 389 Trophy V-8 engine options were available ranging from a 230 horsepower economy version to a 348 horsepower Tri-Power bully. Little known, and even less understood, were the sixteen 421 Super Duty Grand Prix hardtops, cars offering race-ready brute force dressed in a classy package suited for a night on the town. This burgundy 1962 Super Duty Grand Prix is the only documented survivor. All sixteen 421 SD Grand Prix models were equipped with steel front clips.

minum. Also keeping the weight down were optional aluminum exhaust manifolds and a special frame. The frame was modified by cutting out sections of the perimeter rails, transforming rectangular tubes into channel. At the track, all this Super Duty equipment translated into a 13.9-second quarter-mile pass at 107mph. "Acceleration figures like these are not uncommon in Super/Stock classes on our drag strips," wrote Huntington. "But when you can turn them with a car just the way you buy it, you have something to scream about."

If Huntington thought the 1962 Super Duty was something to shout about, the 1963 rendi-

A special, finned, blacked-out rear cove panel represented the quickest way to identify a 1962 Grand Prix from the rear. Pontiac's popular, optional eight-lug rims were installed on fourteen of the sixteen Super Grand Prix sport coupes. Total 1962 Grand Prix production was 30,195.

Pontiac's vaunted 405 horsepower 421 Super Duty was fed by two Carter AFB four-barrels on an aluminum intake. Total flow for the twin Carters was about 1000cfm. The intake had no provision for exhaust warm-up (keeping the fuel mixture cool provided maximum volumetric efficiency), contributing to the Super Duty's cantankerous nature on the street. According to *Motor Trend*'s Roger Huntington, "you can get there and back [in a Super Duty], but it's like driving a racing car in traffic."

tion would have had him hollering his head off. It was slated to have more power and even less weight, especially if the car was one of the fourteen or fifteen plexiglass-windowed,"Swiss cheese" A/FX Catalinas (frames were drilled for lightening, thus the Swiss cheese reference). NASCAR variants of the 1963 Super Duty

Right
Contributing to the 1962 Grand Prix's sporty image were standard bucket seats and a console. Choosing the optional four-speed stick further heightened that image. Notice the conspicuously absent radio in the dashboard's center, something uncommon for a Grand Prix but typical in a Super Duty's case.

would have surely helped Pontiac continue its NASCAR domination (twenty-two wins in 1962). But another season on the superspeedways was nipped in the bud by GM officials.

In January 1963, GM's top brass had determined that they had seen enough of Pontiac's, as well as Chevrolet's, performance escapades and sent word to all divisions to cease and desist such shenanigans. A curt memo was delivered to "all zone car distributors" at Pontiac explaining that "effective today, January 24, 1963, 389 and 421 Super Duty engines are canceled and no further orders will be accepted. Suggest you advise dealers who normally handle this type of business verbally." And just like that, the Super Duty tale came to an end, although the name would later return as a Firebird badge of honor in 1973.

Radical, not-ready-for-prime-time performers like the 421 Super Duty cars were gone by mid-1963, and Pontiac's more civilized models were left to temporarily carry on as the division's most muscular offerings. This wasn't all bad considering that hot options like Tri-Power and a more street-worthy 421 High Output (HO) V-8 were still available to the average

stoplight warrior. Also present was the sporty, classy Grand Prix, which had debuted in 1962 as Pontiac's response to Ford's Thunderbird in the four-place, personal-luxury market.

A relatively quick fix, the 1962 Grand Prix was simply a basic Catalina sport coupe with a few trim tricks applied on the outside and standard bucket seats with a console and tachometer inside. Throw in the wonderfully sporty optional eight-lug aluminum wheels, the 333 horsepower 389 Tri-Power V-8, and perhaps a four-speed transmission and you were ready to fly first class. As far as *Motor Trend*'s critics saw it, "style-wise and price-wise [the Grand Prix]

Heavy-duty 15in steel rims were included with the Super Duty's optional heavy-duty brake package, which featured widened 11in aluminum front drums (rears were cast-iron) with cooling fins.

Left
Notice the missing fender script (normally located just behind the headlights) on this black 1962 Catalina. Not all 421 Super Duty Catalinas had aluminum front ends but this one does, and apparently drilling those fragile fenders for the stock script wasn't always performed—some Super Duty Pontiacs have the trim pieces, some don't.

29

competes directly with the Thunderbird. Performance-wise, it's in a class by itself."

A complete Bill Mitchell restyle resulted in a truly refined Grand Prix for 1963. Super clean lines combined with equally clean body sides absent of unnecessary chrome baubles convinced *Car Life*'s crew to call PMD's second Grand Prix "one of the most handsome [cars] ever to come out of a Detroit styling studio." Performance was also attractive thanks to the optional 370 horsepower 421 V-8. In a *Motor Trend* test, a 370 horsepower Grand Prix stormed 0–60 in just 6.6 seconds and required only 8.5 seconds more to complete a quarter-mile—exceptional numbers for a big car loaded down with classy luxury. As *Motor Trend*'s Bob McVay concluded, the 1963 Grand Prix was "designed for the man who likes to go places fast in quiet elegance and luxury."

The slightly face-lifted 1964 Grand Prix offered a nearly identical combination of performance and luxury. Later renditions, however, tended more towards the luxury side as horsepower options were played down and the

Left
**According to Pete McCarthy's fabulous book,
Pontiac Musclecar Performance, 1955-1975,
Pontiac built 213 Super Duty V-8s for 1962, with
thirteen being single-carb 385 horsepower 389s.
Apparently, 179 Super Duty Pontiacs were built
that year: twenty-four Catalina sedans; 139
Catalina hardtops; and, oddly enough, sixteen
luxo-cruiser Grand Prix sport coupes. Of the total,
172 were 405 horsepower 421s, seven were 389s.
The difference between engines built and cars
produced probably involved racing team spares.**

Standard Super Duty exhaust manifolds were large, "long branch" cast-iron headers with individual runners and two openings on the lower end. One typically fed a 2.25in header pipe leading to a low-restriction muffler. The other was this 3in cutout sealed by a bolt-on cover. With the bolts in place, a Super Duty could operate reasonably quietly on the street; unbolting the cover allowed unrestricted wide-open running at the track. Exotic aluminum long branch exhausts were also offered.

cars grew heavier. It wasn't until the downsized G-body Grand Prix debuted in 1969 that real performance would again become a GP feature. Lighter and easier to handle than previous renditions, the 1969 Grand Prix SJ responded well with either the standard 370 horsepower 428 or optional 390 horsepower big-block under its stretched hood. According to *Car Life*, the 390 SJ was capable of a truly hot 14.10-

The 2+2 image simply begged to be complemented by Pontiac's optional eight-lug wheels. PMD's 421 cubic inch big-block V-8 replaced the 389 as the 2+2's standard power source in 1965.

Pontiac designers rarely took a back seat to anyone when it came to sporty interiors. Bucket seats and a console were included as part of the 2+2 deal. Adding the optional custom gauge cluster and four-speed with Hurst shifter and tachometer only helped make things inside a 1965 2+2 all that more exciting.

A 338 horsepower 421 V-8 was standard for the 1965 2+2, with this 421 HO Tri-Power available on the options list. Output was 376 horsepower at 5500rpm. Compression was 10.75:1. Chrome engine dress-up was a standard 2+2 feature.

Standard 1967 Grand Prix power came from a 350 horsepower 400 V-8 with a four-barrel carburetor. Next on the list was a no-cost option, the economical 265 horsepower 400 two-barrel. At the top were two 428s, a 360 horsepower version and this 376 horsepower bruiser. Both 428s received chrome dress-up, with the 376 horsepower V-8 getting an exclusive open-element air cleaner. Notice the optional cruise control equipment at the air cleaner's right.

Chapter 3

A Tiger by the Tail
GTO—Detroit's First Muscle Car

If you wanted a fast American car in the early 1960s, your choices were limited. At that time, big cubes in big cars represented the only way to fly for performance-minded drivers, basically because one size fit all; Detroit built full-sized models and nothing else. Almost. Chevrolet's Corvair, Ford's Falcon, and Plymouth's Valiant had emerged in 1960 to help fend off the foreign compact invasion, but their arrival was of no concern to the hot-blooded buyer hunting the biggest bang for his buck. Equally ignored the following year was the introduction of General Motors' senior compacts, Buick's Special, and Oldsmobile's F-85. These cars were comfortably larger than the groundbreaking Corvair, yet still lacked any real performance potential.

Even less enticing was Pontiac's Tempest, a bona fide budget buggy with its unconventional rear transaxle and "rope" driveshaft (which reduced harmonic vibration) tied to an economical four-cylinder powerplant (created,

simply enough, by cutting Pontiac's 389 cubic inch V-8 in half). A dozen or so 1963 Tempests powered by 421 Super Duty V-8s were specially built for factory experimental (FX) drag racing competition, but this was before GM clamped down on such outrageous behavior. Standard street-going Tempests, optional 326 cubic inch V-8 power notwithstanding, remained as slow as slugs with none of those Super Duty shenanigans ever intended for anyone but professional drag racers.

All that changed in 1964, the year GM introduced its A-bodies, a new class of automobiles. A-bodies picked up where the senior compacts left off, retaining the existing name-

Wearing the same body shell introduced the previous year with its attractive tunneled rear glass design, Pontiac's 1967 GTO received a slightly revised tail treatment that did away with the flared endcaps and traded the triple-louvered taillights for a double rank arrangement.

Pontiac brochures called the 1964 GTO "a device for shrinking time and distance"—today, most performance fans recognize it as Detroit's first muscle car, a machine that successfully combined big-block V-8 power with a light, manageable, mid-sized body. This incorrectly painted 1964 GTO convertible is one of 6,644 built. Hardtops numbered 18,422, coupes 7,384. The twin exhaust tips were a popular option.

plates while they were at it. Soon to be called intermediates, GM's redesigned Special, F-85, and Tempest, along with Chevrolet's all-new Chevelle, were not all that much smaller inside and out than their full-sized brethren, yet they were lighter and more agile. Most important, these mid-sized models could easily handle serious V-8 power, something obviously impossible in the compact Corvair's case and initially a difficult proposition as far as the slightly larger Chevy II Nova was concerned.

Dropping a powerful V-8 in the 1963 Tempest had proven more trouble that it was worth, even though PMD's big 389 V-8 took up no more space than the 326. Engineers Bill Collins and John DeLorean had experimented with a 389-powered Tempest in 1963, but the unit-body/rear-transaxle layout wasn't exactly designed with high performance in mind. Although beefing up the platform may have worked for the few experimental Super Duty Tempests, the modifications required for a regular-production, street-going super Tempest would have never been approved by the guys on the fourteenth floor. Nearly all headaches were cured, however, once the mid-sized 1964 Tempest came along with its full-perimeter frame and conventional solid rear axle.

Not one to overlook a performance opportunity, PMD's ever-present advertising wizard Jim Wangers was already at work with DeLorean on a trend-setting performance package before the ink even dried on the 1964 Tempest's blueprints. DeLorean had the engineering groundwork laid, while Wangers had his finger on the pulse of a youthful market poised to pounce on his powerful proposition. All that remained was to sell the idea of a big-block intermediate to GM's top brass, a task that wouldn't be easy considering the corporation's anti-performance stance, as well its 330 cubic inch maximum displacement limit for the new mid-sized models.

Well aware of these roadblocks, Wangers and DeLorean made an end run. New models required corporate approval, but option packages could be created without a nod from above, leaving a loophole to at least get the project off the ground. From there, it was basically a matter of running until someone told Wangers and DeLorean to stop. Since receiving permission to supersede the 330 cubic inch limit would clearly never come, the best bet was to build a 389 Tempest first and worry about the consequences later. Of course, none of this plan had a prayer without the support of

PMD General Manager Pete Estes. He loved the 389 Tempest idea and went nose-to-nose with GM's disagreeable ivory tower crew over the plan. Without a doubt, it was Estes' perseverance seemingly against all odds that made the project possible.

This optional custom wheel cover with its three-bladed spinner helped to dress up a 1964 GTO. A simulated wire wheel cover was also offered. Original equipment tires, long since gone in this case, were US Royal Tiger Paw redlines, while a whitewall tire could have replaced the redlines at no extra cost.

Bucket seats and an engine-turned dashboard appliqué were standard on the 1964 GTO. Optional equipment appearing here includes the console, Hurst-shifted four-speed manual transmission, 7000rpm tach (in the right-hand instrument pod), vacuum gauge (on the console), and the popular four-spoke, woodgrain Custom Sport steering wheel.

Left
Standard GTO transmission fare in 1964 was a three-speed manual, with the M20 wide-ratio four-speed, M21 close-ratio four-speed, and Powerglide automatic available at extra cost. Manual transmissions all received Hurst shifters. The optional console and vacuum gauge were available with any transmission.

Credit for naming that project went to DeLorean, who chose GTO, a moniker brashly borrowed from Enzo Ferrari. In Italian, GTO stood for "Gran Turismo Omologato" ("Grand Touring Homologated" for all you Yankees). When Ferrari used the name, he meant it—his legendary 1962 250 GTO was built to homologate (legalize) itself for FIA-sanctioned GT racing competition. Not all among the motoring press approved of Pontiac's somewhat shameless attempt to ride the coattails of Ferrari's fabled image.

Referring to Pontiac's tradition of naming vehicles after competition events—Grand Prix and LeMans had already been snapped up by PMD label-makers—*Road & Track*'s critics let loose with both barrels. A March 1964 *R&T* report said it all:

These thefts were bad enough . . . displaying the intention of the company to trade on an image that was not deserved and had not been earned. Now, however, Pontiac has gone even further, lifting the exact designation of a highly successful GT racing car, the GTO, from Ferrari. There is an unforgivable dishonesty in such a practice as this and the insult should be sufficient to prevent any intelligent person from regarding it with anything except derision.

Car and Driver's David E. Davis disagreed wholeheartedly, even going so far as to bark-up a Ferrari GTO versus Pontiac GTO shoot-out on the cover of his magazine's March 1964 issue. While *Road & Track* was pointing out that Pontiac's GTO was certainly no match for its Ferrari counterpart, Davis was pointing out that such a comparison was akin to squaring off apples and oranges. While the Ferrari would lose in a drag race, the Pontiac was no match on a European road course. "Ferrari never built enough GTOs to earn the name anyway," wrote Davis, "just to be on the safe side though, Pontiac built a faster one."

Officially released on October 1, 1963, Pontiac's GTO debuted, per Wangers' ploy, as an option package for the deluxe Tempest model, the aforementioned LeMans. Initially, it was available for the LeMans sports coupe and convertible and was joined soon after introduction by a hardtop. The GTO options package included a 325 horsepower 389 big-block V-8 featuring a hydraulic cam, a Carter AFB four-barrel, and a pair of high-compression heads borrowed from the 389's big brother, the 421. Stiffer suspension, a three-speed manual with a Hurst shifter, and various dress-up items including a blacked-out grille, GTO identification, and twin dummy scoops on the hood were also part of the deal. Popular options included a Muncie four-speed, a limited-slip Safe-T-Track differential, and an even hotter 348 horsepower 389 topped by three Rochester two-barrel carbs.

Armed with the optional 348 horsepower V-8 and 3.90:1 rear gears, a 1964 GTO could trip the lights at the drag strip's far end in 14.30 seconds according to *Popular Hot Rodding*. As *Car and Driver*'s Davis saw it, the new GTO "does what so many others only talk about—it

The 1966 GTO's louvered taillights, flared rear-quarter endcaps, and Coke bottle body were welcomed styling improvements. Convertible production in 1966 was 12,798; 10,363 coupes and 73,785 hardtops were also built.

really does combine brute, blasting performance with balance and stability of a superior nature."

Inspiration for Davis' raves were two 1964 Royal Bobcat GTOs specially prepared by Roy-

Left
Pontiac reshaped its A-body for 1966, creating a less angular GTO, again offered in coupe, hardtop, and convertible form. This year it was offered as a model series all its own instead of an option package for the LeMans. After selling 75,352 Goats in 1965, Pontiac hit a peak in 1966 as GTO production reached 96,946.

al Pontiac—PMD's backdoor performance dealership—using various hot stock parts, as well as a tuning tweak or two. In *Car and Driver*'s test, a Royal Bobcat GTO screamed from rest to 60mph in 4.6 seconds. Quarter-mile performance was listed as 13.1 seconds at 115mph. Non-stock test subjects aside, it was Davis' GTO review that helped vault both his magazine and Pontiac's new performance machine into the forefront.

Thanks to the boldness of Estes, Wangers, and DeLorean, Pontiac had become the first mainstream manufacturer to combine brute, large-displacement power with a relatively lightweight body, a practice that would soon escalate throughout Detroit. GTO copies quickly followed, cars like Buick's Gran Sport, Oldsmobile's 4-4-2, and Chevrolet's Chevelle SS 396.

Advertisements described PMD's GTO as a tiger; average Joes affectionately called it the "Goat." Popular hit records sang its praises. As for critics and complainers on GM's fourteenth floor, they were silenced once sales started to soar. The GTO would have undoubtedly stood as the star of Detroit's 1964 show had not Ford chosen the same year to introduce its Mustang, a mass-market marvel if there ever was one. But while the wildly successful Mustang became everyone's darling, the GTO, as David

The GTO's fabled Tri-Power setup, its top performance option since the car's 1964 inception, made its last appearance in 1966. Effective for the 1967 model year, GM officials canceled multi-carb equipment for all models except Chevrolet's Corvette. These three Rochester two-barrels helped the GTO's 389 big-block pump out 360 horsepower. Compression was 10.75:1. Tri-Power production in 1966 was 19,045.

E. Davis wrote in 1975, "appeared on the American scene like a Methodist minister leaving a massage parlor."

The GTO's first-year success inspired Pontiac officials to project production of 50,000 for the second-edition version in 1965. They missed their mark, however, as sales eventually surpassed 75,352. A revised front end exchanged 1964's horizontal quad headlights for a stacked arrangement, and a slight power boost came courtesy of an upgraded cam and improved intake. Still an option for the three LeMans models, the 1965 GTO package contained a standard 335 horsepower 389 four-barrel, with the Tri-Power version now rated at 360 horses.

New extra-cost features included "Rally Cluster" instrumentation, Rally wheels (supplied by Kelsey Hayes), and an air scoop package, released on August 17, 1965. The first in a long line of GTO Ram Air equipment, the air scoop package was offered over dealer counters only for Tri-Power models. Ram Air made the restyled 1965 hood's distinctive single scoop fully functional by sealing the three Rochesters' small air cleaners to the hood's underside using a special tub topped by a large foam gasket.

Whether in standard trim or fully loaded, the 1965 GTO continued to impress. "In all, the GTO is a fun-to-drive machine," wrote *Hot Rod's* Eric Dahlquist. "Success formulas are elusive creatures at best but Pontiac seems to have at least part of the market cornered for the time being." Mincing fewer words after his turn trying to hold Pontiac's tiger, *Car Craft's* LeRoi

The 1966 dashboard was similar in layout to the 1965 GTO's four-pod panel, but came standard with a woodgrain face. The walnut shift knob, like the Hurst four-speed stick it's threaded on, was an optional piece in 1966.

Smith concluded, "as a total driving impression, handling the GTO is best described as WILD!"

Fueled by even more success, Pontiac's brain trust decided to transform the GTO into a model series all its own for 1966. Revamped A-body sheet metal was also supplied, with a similar split-grille/stacked-headlight nose mated to an updated shell that hinted slightly at a Coke bottle shape. In back was a definitely different tail treatment featuring louvered taillights. Appearing fresh while still looking much like the original, the 1966 model ended up as Pontiac's most popular GTO with sales topping out at 96,946.

Power levels carried over identically from 1965 with one major exception. Quietly released in February 1966, the XS-code Tri-Power 389 featured an even stronger cam, stiffer valve springs and the functional air scoop package introduced in 1965. Ordering the XS 389 also meant adding the M21 close-ratio four-speed, heavy-duty fan, metallic brakes, and 4.33:1 limited-slip differential, all mandatory options. Estimates put production of XS-equipped 1966 GTOs at about 185.

While looking much the same on the outside—save for a slightly restructured tail,

The 14in Rally wheel—introduced in 1965—carried over as an option for the 1966 GTO. Standard 1966 GTO wheels were 14x6in stamped steel rims with wheel covers. Simulated wire wheel covers and deluxe wheel covers were again available on the options list.

enlarged rocker brightwork, and a mesh grille—Pontiac's 1967 GTO differed considerably from its 1966 predecessor underneath. For starters, the venerable 389 was bored out to 400ci and the famed Tri-Power option was dropped as GM vetoed multiple carburetor setups for all models but the Corvette after 1966.

In all, four varieties of the 400 big-block were offered, beginning with a standard four-barrel version rated at 335 horsepower. Buyers who preferred a little less oomph could opt, at no extra cost, for a milder, low-compression 255 horsepower 400 topped by a two-barrel carburetor. On the other side of the coin was the HO 400, an engine that also carried a familiar rating of 360 horsepower. Top of the heap was the Ram Air 400, again conservatively rated at 360 horsepower like its 1966 XS Tri-Power predecessor. Much of the 1966 XS equipment carried over with new additions being the HO's free-flowing exhaust manifolds and a Quadra-Jet four-barrel instead of the three Rochesters. Late in the year, better heads with revised valves and springs were also added. According to *Motor Trend*, this equipment could help propel a 1967 GTO to a 14.21-second quarter-mile pass.

Also of note was a new optional transmission, GM's three-speed Turbo Hydra-Matic,

**Right
The distinctive wire mesh grille and large, bright rocker trim set the 1967 GTO apart from its 1966 predecessor as sheet metal carried over in basically identical fashion. Pontiac built 9,517 1967 convertibles.**

A slight overbore upped the GTO's displacement ante from 389 to 400 cubic inches for 1967. Standard power came from this 335 horsepower 400 four-barrel V-8, with a low compression (8.6:1) two-barrel "economy" version offered at no extra cost. Compression for the 335 horsepower big-block remained at 10.75:1.

which replaced the aged two-speed Power-glide. And when auto trans GTO buyers also checked off the optional console, they got the innovative Dual Gate shifter, yet another popular Goat feature supplied by Hurst. Known as the His and Hers stick, the Hurst Dual Gate allowed the driver to chose between conventional automatic transmission operation or manual selection of shift points. Demonstrating the merits of both the Turbo Hydra-Matic and the His and Hers shifter, production of auto-

matic-equipped GTOs surpassed their manual trans counterparts for the first time.

GM's killjoys got their way at the end of the 1966 model run and canceled the popular "GeeTO Tiger" ad campaigns that had reportedly incited unacceptable behavior among this country's driving youth, at least according to Ralph Nader and the Federal Trade Commission. Accordingly, in 1967, Pontiac's GTO became "The Great One" as safety consciousness, federally mandated or otherwise, began to take root in the muscle car realm.

Big news for 1968 came in the form of a totally restyled, rounded body featuring hideaway wipers and an innovative energy-absorbing bumper up front. Reportedly, the color-keyed plastic Endura nose could survive minor impacts and spring back to its original form within twenty-four hours. Optional hideaway headlights and an eye-catching hood tach (first offered in 1967) only helped sweeten the appearance. Inside, the 1968 GTO's redesigned three-pod dash layout was, in *Hot Rod* magazine's terms, "the best instrument panel in super-car-land." Overall, the fifth-edition Goat remained at the head of Detroit's muscle car pack—as PMD ads claimed "others have caught on, but they haven't caught up."

Again, four 400 big-blocks were available under the 1968 GTO's hood, which reverted back to the original twin-scoop style. Still at the top, at least early in the model run, was the 360 horsepower 400 Ram Air V-8. In March 1968, the Ram Air 400 was replaced by the Ram Air II, an improved 400 with a beefed-up crank, forged pistons, larger pushrods, and new heads featuring revised combustion chambers, rounder ports, and lighter valves. Output for the Ram Air II remained at 360 horsepower.

Building a better Goat remained basically an underhood affair for 1969 as outward appearances carried over with only minor modifications—but what a job Pontiac engineers did beneath those scoops. While powertrain choices once more numbered four, the 400 HO was dropped in favor of a 366 horsepower Ram Air 400, since labeled the Ram Air

III. Ram Air III features included improved heads with D ports and free-flowing exhausts.

Even more impressive was the new Ram Air IV 400, a radical 370 horsepower big-block with large-port heads, a lumpier cam, low-restriction exhausts and a Rochester Quadra-Jet four-barrel on an aluminum intake. According to *Car Life*, the Ram Air IV was "a very peaky engine. The idle is a rough, rolling bark, music to the driver's ears and a warning to people in

The 1967 GTO's interior again incorporated the woodgrain touch. New for the year was Hurst's innovative "His and Hers" Dual Gate shifter. The His and Hers stick was connected to the equally new three-speed Turbo Hydra-Matic automatic transmission and offered a choice between typical automatic operation or manual shifting. Outnumbered two to one in previous years, automatic-equipped GTOs surpassed manual models by about 3,000 in 1967, a trend that continued with every Goat to follow. The underdash gauges are non-stock owner-installed items.

the next lane." Mandatory Ram Air IV options included a choice between a 3.90:1 or 4.33:1 Safe-T-Track rear end and a heavy-duty radiator.

Along with the Ram Air IV, Pontiac also introduced The Judge for 1969. Initially meant to be a bare-bones GTO comparable to Plymouth's budget-minded Road Runner, PMD's Judge was actually introduced with a few more frills than planned, though as a $332 GTO

This five-spoke Rally II sport wheel, featuring bright trim rings and color-keyed lug nuts, joined the optional Rally wheel in 1967.

option, it would have been tough to find a bigger bang for the buck. Included in The Judge deal was a 366 horsepower Ram Air III 400, a Hurst-shifted three-speed, heavy-duty suspension, Rally II wheels (without trim rings), and various exterior dress-up (rear deck spoiler, body side tape stripe, and The Judge decals). Also available at extra cost was the intimidating Ram Air IV. The first 2,000 Judges off the line were painted Carousel Red, with paint choices expanding to any GTO color after February 1969. Judge production continued through 1971.

GTO advancements for 1970 included a revised nose and tail and an anti-sway bar added to the rear suspension. Under the hood, the low-compression 400 two-barrel V-8 was dropped just in time to make way for Pontiac's 455 cubic inch big-block. Before 1970, 400ci had been the limit for GM's A-bodies, but that barrier came down just as the corporation's intermediates were gaining some serious weight. Joining the Ram Air III and IV on the GTO options list, the torquey 360 horsepower 455 was really no match for its smaller 400 cubic inch running mates, a fact pointed out by *Car and Driver*'s staff, who called Pontiac's biggest big-block a "low-revving device that makes very little ruckus."

With the handwriting on the wall, the 1971 GTO rolled out with yet another new nose and even lower compression under the hood. Like the dinosaurs before them, the Ram Air V-8s were history, superseded by the 335 horsepower 455 HO. Standard power came from a 300 horsepower 400. Clearly indicative of the

A totally new body helped boost GTO production from 81,722 in 1967 to 87,684 in 1968, the second highest total in the eleven-year Goat run. The hideaway headlights were optional, but so many 1968 GTO buyers opted for this trendy feature that most innocent bystanders thought them standard. While the twin-scooped hood was a throwback to the original GTO rendition, the innovative, color-keyed Endura front end was typical of Pontiac's state-of-the-art design tradition.

times, GTO production dropped from 40,149 in 1970 to only 10,532 in 1971. That downhill slide continued as emissions controls, safety-conscious legislation, and intimidating insurance rates finally succeeded in bringing the muscle car crowd to its collective knees. In 1972, the GTO again became an optional LeMans package and a coupe reappeared as the convertible was dropped. Total 1972 production was a mere 5,807.

With Pontiac concentrating on its Firebird Trans Am, the GTO was left to flounder in the shadows, first as an almost overlooked option on the totally restyled 1973 LeMans, then as another optional package on the little 1974 Ventura—the first and only time a GTO would rely on small-block power. Although reasonably attractive and somewhat intriguing, the Ventura GTO just didn't fill the bill, and it was only right to bring the once-proud bloodline to an end.

Pontiac's popular Rally II wheels appeared yet again as a GTO option in 1968, as did a choice between standard US Royal redline or whitewall tires. Wider G70 rubber was an option as well.

Standard power for the 1968 GTO was boosted up to 350 horsepower in 1968. The low-compression, two-barrel 400 big-block was again offered at no extra cost, this time rated at 265 horsepower. Discriminating performance buyers could order the optional 360 horsepower 400 HO, shown here equipped with the over-the-counter Ram Air induction setup. Available only as a dealer-installed option (shipped in the trunk) through 1968, the Ram Air induction equipment became a true factory option in 1969.

F errari never built enough GTOs to earn the name anyway, just to be on the safe side though, Pontiac built a faster one.

—*Car and Driver,*
March 1964

Previous pages
Introduced in December 1968, with actual production beginning in January 1969, The Judge was initially offered as a budget-minded performance package for the GTO priced at $332. Borrowing a popular image from television's Rowan and Martin comedy team ("Here come da' judge . . . "), Pontiac's brain trust originally envisioned a performance car with few frills. Relatively speaking, the first Judge in 1968 had few frills even with its standard rear spoiler and Judge graphics. The following year, however, PMD's Judge was adorned with even splashier graphics The performance imagery carried over to 1971 as exemplified by this 1971 Judge hardtop.

The hood-mounted 8000rpm tach, first offered in 1967, was a popular option that perfectly suited The Judge image.

Rally II wheels without trim rings (to keep costs down) were standard Judge features from the beginning. This 1971 Judge hardtop is one of only 357 built, thanks to the model being discontinued midyear. A mere seventeen 1971 Judge convertibles were built.

Along with all that reflective striping, Judges from 1969 to 1971 also received a standard rear wing. Notice the engine identification on the wing, a relocation required since "The Judge" decal occupied the typical engine decal front fender location. Judge hardtop production was 6,725 in 1969 and 3,629 in 1970. Another 108 convertibles were built in 1969, followed by 168 the following year.

Other than "The Judge" glovebox identification and the Hurst shifter's T-handle, the 1971 Judge interior was identical to the standard 1971 GTO's.

The optional Formula steering wheel, first used as a 1969 Trans Am feature, had become an extra-cost GTO feature in 1970.

Left
All 1971 Judge models were equipped with the 335 horsepower 455 HO V-8 and Ram Air. In 1970, the 455 big-block had become a Judge option late in the year, joining the Ram Air III (standard) and Ram Air IV (optional) 400s.

A UAW strike in 1970 delayed the appearance of GM's totally restyled A-body until 1973, meaning Pontiac ended up breaking its traditional two-year styling cycle in 1972, relying on the same shell for the third straight year. Total 1972 GTO production was only 5,807, counting 134 coupes. For the first time, Pontiac did not produce a GTO convertible.

The idle is a rough, rolling bark, music to the driver's ears and a warning to people in the next lane.

—*Car Life*
on the Ram Air IV engine

GTO power choices numbered three in 1972: the standard 250 horsepower 400, the 250 horsepower L78 455, and the 300 horsepower LS5 455 HO. The L78 455 big-block was only offered with the Turbo Hydra-Matic automatic. This Cardinal Red 1972 GTO hardtop, which sports the 1971-style rear valance and twin exhaust outlets, is one of only 325 equipped with the 455 HO V-8 and automatic transmission.

Chapter 4

Pontiac's Pony Cars
High-Flying Firebirds

In General Motors' terms, its newest platform was known as the F-body, a small car with a long hood and short rear deck that was similar to Ford's incredibly popular Mustang. The similarity between Dearborn's pony car progenitor and Chevrolet's impending F-body was no mere coincidence. Roughly four months after the Mustang had kicked off the breed in April 1964, GM chiefs sent the word down from the fourteenth floor to develop direct competition. Chevy designers wasted little time copying Ford's record-setting formula. Per parameters already established by the Mustang, GM's pony car would be sporty, practical, and affordable. And also like its Ford rival, the new F-body would offer its fair share of performance potential.

On September 29, 1966, Chevrolet rolled out a pony car legend of its own: the Camaro. The race-bred Z/28 followed early in 1967, and the rest is history—few American performance machines can brag of careers as long

and successful as Chevy's hot little F-body. But in terms of uninterrupted service, one macho machine stands above the Z/28, and again by no coincidence it, too, is a GM F-body.

Introduced February 23, 1967, Pontiac's Firebird hit the streets running and has never stopped. Two years later, PMD rolled out its famed Trans Am variant, a spirited, splashy road warrior that has managed to survive oil embargoes, restrictive emissions standards, and safety legislation to become Detroit's only 1960s muscle car legend offered nonstop every year from its debut to the present. (Chevy's Z/28 took leave after 1974 and returned as a midyear model in 1977.) And to think Pontiac

Essentially identical from 1970 to 1973, Pontiac's Trans Am was only offered with one powerplant, the 455 HO, in 1971 and 1972. This Trans Am is one of only 458 built in 1972 with a manual transmission; another 828 rolled out the door with automatics, a no-cost option.

That distinctive split-grille Pontiac nose, in concert with the Firebird 400's attractive twin-scoop hood, made mistaking PMD's first F-body for its Camaro cousin impossible. Popular Firebird options included the hood tach and 14in Rally II wheels (an $84.26 option for the 1967 Firebird). The Rally IIs on this Firebird are incorrect 15in versions, and the rear traction bars are non-stock owner additions.

people almost had to be dragged kicking and screaming into the pony car corral.

PMD General Manager John DeLorean had liked the idea of a small, sporty Pontiac, but in no way did he want Chevy's F-body leftovers. Having risen to the general manager's post in July 1965 after Pete Estes moved to Chevrolet, DeLorean was still a performance-minded engineer at heart. He harbored visions of a true Pontiac sports car, a dream both he and Estes had been considering since early 1963. DeLorean's ideal involved two seats, fiberglass bodywork, four-wheel independent suspension and Euro-style six-cylinder power—a low-priced Corvette of sorts. A clay model of his XP-833 prototype, later named the Banshee, first saw light in August 1964, about the time GM officials were giving the go-ahead for Chevrolet's F-body Panther project. Rolling XP-833 test beds followed in the fall as DeLorean stood steadfast—to hell with the F-body, his Banshee would be ready for production by 1967.

DeLorean's far-fetched Banshee never really had a prayer of following in the Goat's footprints as a proposal-turned-production-reality-despite-disapproval-from-the-fourteenth floor. Enough smart men at GM knew the GTO would sell in 1964; a few years later, many of those same people recognized the Banshee as a certified lead balloon. Nonetheless, DeLorean continued lobbying for his sports car and designers were sculpting on his ideal as late as February 1966, even as work on Pontiac's version of GM's F-body was progressing.

Fed up with DeLorean's persistence, GM Executive Vice President Ed Cole laid down the

Best quarter-mile performance (14.03 seconds at 103.6mph) for a 1967 Firebird 400 was recorded by *Super Stock & Drag Illustrated's* testers. Total 1967 Firebird 400 production, coupe and convertible, was 18,632.

law in March 1966, informing PMD's general manager to forget the Banshee and "make a car out of the Camaro." Although time was short and there wasn't all that much PMD's design crew could do to separate their F-body from Chevy's Camaro, they managed to inject enough Pontiac flair into the new pony car to give it its own identity.

Named after GM's experimental turbine cars of 1954, 1956, and 1958, Pontiac's Firebird emerged looking, understandably, much like a Camaro in the middle. Simple modifications in back helped set it apart, but the real

This fully loaded black beauty features the optional Rally II wheels, E70x14in redline tires, **"HO" body side stripe, and Pontiac's trademark twin-split exhaust tips.**

difference came up front where Pontiac's traditional split-grille theme was applied in particularly attractive fashion. Measuring 5in longer than a Camaro's nose, the Firebird front end offered a much more pleasing facade than the one applied to Chevy's F-body.

After selling 82,560 F-bodies in 1967, Pontiac returned with a basically identical Firebird package for 1968. Total sales grew to 107,112, including 16,960 convertibles. This droptop 1968 Firebird 400 is one of only 2,087 (coupe and convertible) built with the 400 HO V-8.

Even so, many among the automotive press were initially cool to the new Firebird. *Car and Driver* characterized it as a "last-minute Camaro conversion" and went on to report:

It was immediately apparent that a reasonably successful job had been done in giving the Firebird a personality of its own, although in profile it is barely distinguishable from a Camaro. We are confident that next year, with several months to shape the F-body to their own requirements, Pontiac's Firebird has an excellent chance of turning into a wholly distinctive member of the Detroit sporty-car set.

What critics couldn't deny, however, was that the Firebird was initially superior to the Camaro beneath the skin, thanks to an engineering tweak or two developed too late to make Chevy's F-body lineup. The Firebird's engine was located farther back than the Camaro's, improving weight balance, while rear springs were reinforced with radius rod traction bars to combat axle hop under hard

Firebirds were both boulevard cruisers and strong street performers. This 400 HO-powered 1968 carries a wide range of Pontiac options, including the close-ratio four-speed transmission with its Hurst shifter and custom walnut shift knob. Also present are air conditioning, power steering and brakes, and console with Rally clock.

acceleration. Overall, the Firebird was a better handler than its F-body cousin, a plain fact that grew even more noticeable once options started piling on. In *Motor Trend*'s words, "a Firebird with heavy-duty components will execute a tight corner like a young Curtis Turner on a moonlight run."

Pontiac's 1967 Firebird debuted as five distinct models delineated by underhood power. PMD ads announced that "The Magnificent Five are here," and bragged that "you'd expect Pontiac to come up with a nifty new sports car like this. But did you expect five?" Reflecting DeLorean's ideals, the lineup began with two Firebirds equipped with Pontiac's innovative overhead-cam six-cylinder, the hottest of the two being the Sprint. Standard Sprint features included the 215 horsepower 230 cubic inch OHV six, a floor shifter, and special "road hugging" suspension.

Next came the V-8s, a mundane 250 horsepower 326, followed by a lively 285 horsepower small-block for the "light heavyweight" Firebird HO. Pontiac's real heavyweight was its Firebird 400, armed with a 325 horsepower punch. An additional $616 added the Ram Air option, which made the Firebird 400's typically Pontiac twin hood scoops fully functional. Although maximum output for the Ram Air 400 remained at 325 horsepower, those horses came on at 5200rpm, 400 higher than the base 400 big-block. According to *Car and Driver*, quarter-mile performance for the Ram Air Firebird 400 was a healthy 14.4 seconds at 100mph.

Basically unchanged from 1967 on the outside, Pontiac's 1968 Firebird was updated

Introduced as both a GTO and Firebird option in 1967, this 8000rpm hood tach was a $63.19 option in 1968.

underneath with multi-leaf rear springs (replacing the 1967's single-leaf units) and staggered rear shocks to further combat axle hop. Underhood revamps included upgrading the base 326 V-8 to a 265 horsepower 350 cubic inch small-block. The 350 HO version was rated at 320 horsepower. Meanwhile, increased compression helped boost the base 400 up five horsepower and the Ram Air V-8 up ten. Also rated at 335 horsepower was a new big-block, the 400 HO. In March 1968, the existing Ram Air 400 was replaced by the 340 horsepower Ram Air II featuring revised heads, forged crank and pistons, and a more aggressive cam.

Firebird styling updates for 1969 included Mercedes 300SL-like fender scoops and an innovative, color-keyed Lexan nose. Underhood affairs for the Firebird 400 basically carried over from 1968 with the exception of the

The 400 High Output (HO) was a new power option introduced for the 1968 Firebird and priced at $350.72. Horsepower was listed at 335, five more than the standard 400 thanks to a more aggressive cam. Compression was 10.75:1.

even stronger Ram Air IV big-block, an $832 option that featured an aluminum intake, better-flowing heads, and 1.65:1 rocker arms.

But of course the really big news for 1969 was the somewhat quiet March introduction of Pontiac's first Trans Am, a potentially high-profile performer that, unlike its prominently promoted GTO Judge sibling, was rolled out with next to no fanfare. Priced at $1,100, the WS4 "Trans Am Performance and Appearance" package went basically overlooked in its debut year. In all, only 697 first-year Trans Ams were built, including eight highly-prized convertibles.

Included in the WS4 package was the 335 horsepower 400 HO (or Ram Air III) backed by a three-speed manual, heavy-duty suspension, 3.55:1 Safe-T-Track differential, power front discs, variable-ratio power steering, F70x14in fiberglass-belted tires, and an exclusive, functional scooped hood (per Ram Air specs). The distinctive front fender scoops were also functional as engine compartment air extractors, as was the large rear airfoil. Polar White paint with blue racing stripes and unobtrusive "Trans Am" identification on the fenders and rear wing topped things off. Optional equipment included, among other things, the 345 horsepower Ram Air IV 400, the M20 or M21 four-speeds, and the Turbo Hydra-Matic automatic. Although few apparently noticed, the package represented an exceptionally attractive send-off for the long-running first-generation design.

As was the case with Chevrolet's Camaro, delays getting the totally new F-body to market for 1970 meant some remaining 1969 Firebirds, including Trans Ams, were sold as 1970 models. When the all-new 1970-1/2 models were finally introduced at the Chicago Auto Show in February 1970, most agreed that the wait was well worth it. Sleek, sexy, and modern, the 1970-1/2 Firebird design was suited only for one bodystyle, a quasi-fastback, leaving a convertible model in the past.

New for 1970 was the Formula 400 with its beefy suspension, rear sway bar, 330 horsepower 400 big-block, and that distinctive "dual-snorkel" fiberglass hood. Per Pontiac tradition, adding the optional 345 horsepower Ram Air III 400 made those two imposing scoops fully functional.

A step above the Formula was the second-generation Trans Am, which, unlike its predecessor, left little doubt about its presence. Featuring a fully functional body package incorporating a rear ducktail spoiler, a new set of front fender air extractors, wheelhouse air deflectors, a rear-facing "shaker" hood scoop, and a front air dam (an item strongly suggested by *Sports Car Graphic*'s testers in 1969), the new Trans Am looked every bit as hot as it ran. Standard power came from the 345 horsepower Ram Air III, with the 370 horsepower Ram Air IV available at extra cost.

From 1971 to 1973, Pontiac's Trans Am rolled on in almost identical fashion on the outside, with a few changes coming beneath that vibrating scoop. Only one big-block, a 455 cubic inch V-8, was offered for the 1971 and 1972 Trans Ams, and it was also included as a Formula option. In 1971, the 455 HO was pegged at 335 horsepower. When net ratings became vogue the following year, HO output dropped to 300 horses. The net-rated 455 HO dropped again in 1973, to 250 horsepower, but a hot, new option appeared to at least partially stem the power drain.

Reaching back to Pontiac performance's outrageous heydays in the early 1960s, PMD engineers dusted off the Super Duty designa-

Following pages
Unlike the redesigned 1968 GTO with its Endura front end, the slightly restyled 1969 Firebird relied on a Lexan nose. Facing increased competition in the pony car field, Pontiac officials watched as 1969 Firebird sales dipped slightly to 87,708. Convertibles numbered 11,649.

tion for a specially prepared 455 introduced early in 1973. Available for both the Trans Am and the Formula, the 455 Super Duty initially pumped out 310 net horses, although an emissions-mandated cam change quickly dropped that figure to 290 horsepower. Included in the 455 SD lineup was a beefy block with four-bolt main bearing caps, a forged-steel crank, and excellent heads with large, round ports.

At a time when the days of the great American muscle car were numbered, Pontiac's 455 SD Trans Am served as a final performance salute, rolling out one last time in 1974 before Pontiac discontinued the 455 under F-body hoods. Called "the last of the fast cars" by *Car and Driver*, the 1973 455 SD Trans Am came "standard with the sort of acceleration that hasn't been seen in years." Quarter-mile performance was listed as 13.8 seconds at 108mph. "Just when we had fast cars relegated to the museum sections," continued *Car and*

Driver's report, "Pontiac has surprised everyone and opened a whole new exhibit." Reportedly, 252 455 SD Trans Ams were built for 1973, followed by 943 in 1974. Forty-three 1973 and fifty-eight 1974 Super Duty Formulas were also produced.

It was only right that Pontiac engineers saved the best of the big-block Trans Ams for last. Although both the Formula and Trans Am carried on into the lukewarm 1980s, it was just never the same after the Super Duty 455 came and went. But at least Pontiac had been among the last of Detroit's auto makers to give up on brute-force performance.

The Trans Am was a little-known Firebird option when introduced in March 1969. Only 697 were built, 634 with the standard L74 400 HO and 55 with the optional L67 Ram Air IV 400. Eight convertibles, all with the L74, were also produced. Loaded with functional body parts—air extractors on the fenders, scoops on the hood, an airfoil in back—the 1969 Trans Am still left *Sports Car Graphic*'s test drivers slightly disappointed. Their report complained of front end lift at highway speeds, and they wished for a front air dam. At the strip, they drove Pontiac's first Trans Am through the quarter-mile lights in 14.3 seconds.

Although steel rims and small hubcaps were standard, almost all of the rarely seen 1969 Trans Am Firebirds have the optional Rally II wheels.

Available in only one color, Polar White, the 1969 Trans Am exterior was complemented by twin blue racing stripes and a matching rear cove panel. Pontiac borrowed the Trans Am name from the Sports Car Club of America racing class , but when SCCA officials threatened to sue over the usage, Pontiac agreed to pay a royalty of $5 per car sold.

Pontiac's second-edition Trans Am featured a truly sporty interior as standard equipment. Included were bucket seats, an engine-turned dash insert, Rally gauges, an 8000rpm tachometer, and the distinctive Formula steering wheel. Choosing the M20 or M21 four-speeds typically added a Hurst shifter. Only 1,339 Trans Ams were ordered with the Turbo Hydra-Matic automatic in 1970.

According to Pontiac's promotional people, the new Trans Am nose with its front air dam and fender-mounted air extractors created 50lb of down force at highway speeds. In *Car & Driver*'s words, the machine was "a hard-muscled, lightning-reflexed commando of a car, the likes of which doesn't exist anywhere in the world, even for twice the price." The ever-present Rally II wheels, without trim rings, were standard features. Only 3,196 1970-1/2 Trans Ams were built, including eighty-eight with the optional Ram Air IV 400.

The all-out Ram Air V 400 began life in 1969 as a destroked 303 cubic inch big-block intended for SCCA Trans Am competition. Rules at the time placed a 305 cubic inch limit on race-legal stock engines. The Ram Air V was never included in a regular production Pontiac for sale to the public. After Pontiac failed to build the 1,000 planned Ram Air V Firebirds in 1969, SCCA officials did away with the limit, allowing PMD engineers to continue work on a 400 cubic inch tunnel-port Ram Air V that reportedly dynoed in the 475 to 525 horsepower range. Again, regular production was planned but fell victim to changing attitudes. Offered only over dealers' counters for a brief time, the Ram Air V 400 made it into public hands as a "crate" motor to be installed by the owner.

Right
The distinctive, twin-scooped Formula 400 joined the Trans Am in Pontiac's pony car performance ranks for 1970. Total 1970 Formula production was 7,708, with this model being one of only 293 built with the 340 horsepower Ram Air III 400 backed by the Turbo Hydra-Matic automatic transmission. Testing a base 330 horsepower Formula 400 with automatic trans and 3.08:1 rear gears, *Car Life's* hotfoots managed a 14.86-second/95.5mph quarter-mile pass.

Choosing either the Ram Air III or Ram Air IV 400 made the Formula's large, twin scoops functional. Beneath these scoops is the Ram Air III big-block, which produced 345 horsepower at 5000rpm; the Ram Air IV pumped out 370 horses at 5500rpm.

Right
In exchange for $94.79, a Formula 400 buyer in 1970 could add the same Rally Gauge Cluster tach/clock combination offered as standard equipment to Trans Am customers.

B ack when the Chisholm
Trail was considered an
express way, you needed 355
horses to haul the mail. We
figure you still do.

—1969 Pontiac advertisement

Previous page
From 1970 to 1972, Trans Ams were only offered
in two colors: Cameo White (Polar White for
1970) and Lucerne Blue. In 1973, Lucerne Blue
was dropped, and Buccaneer Red and Brewster
Green were added.

When first offered in 1971, Pontiac's honeycomb
wheel was listed as being available for all Firebirds
except the Trans Ams. The 15in Rally II wheel
(without trim rings at this point) was the TA
standard. Later in 1971, however, the
honeycombs were listed as a $36.86 Trans Am
option.

The standard 1972 Trans Am interior carried over basically unchanged from 1970. Optional equipment appearing here includes power door locks, power windows, AM/FM stereo, and air conditioning.

Were Pontiac designers optimistic or what? Detroit's speedometers didn't read much faster than the Trans Am's 160mph unit.

Right
Using Detroit's new SAE net rating system, Pontiac engineers advertised the 1972 Trans Am's 455 HO as producing 300 maximum net horsepower at 4000rpm. Basically the same 8.4:1 compression big-block offered at 335 gross horsepower the year before, the 1972 455 HO also produced 415lb of torque at 3200rpm.

Index